Table Arrangements

Table arrangements are made of flowers, botanical and artificial materials.
They are arranged in one or several containers by means of a supporting medium.
Various techniques are applied, according to the specific needs of the material and the emotions
you want to express with your table setting. Water supply is a question of need based on the materials
and the timeframe in which the table setting is being used.

Per, Max and Tomas

Creativity with flowers

Table Arrangements

Per Benjamin
Max van de Sluis
Tomas De Bruyne

Garland

The history of table arrangements

Table arrangements, single flowers in a glass, loosely arranged flowers in a jug or vase or arrangements of different complexity; whatever shape they appear, they are one of the most important floral features in our lives. Flowers spreading comfort, warmth, joy and happiness during our meals. Be it a small dinner with family and friends, dinners celebrating birthdays, anniversaries and any party, or bigger themed event, they are always in focus and missed when absent!

Flowers have been part of our lives throughout the ages, reflecting developments and changes in people's ways of life, historically mostly used by rich nobles in society and, in modern times, spreading down into all strata of society.

Extensive evidence of flower use from ancient times is to be found in simple wall paintings, and on murals, frescos on artefacts and described in writing and paintings. We have evidence of people "arranging" flowers in many ways, in all kinds of containers, vases, pots or anything at hand, single flowers to complex designs.

Early table arrangements consisted of garlands, wreaths and flower petals then came arrangements, being a great mix of what today would be named as bouquets, loosely arranged flowers as well as arrangements, to more advanced installations of grand creativity. To show the etymology of the table arrangement, the various fields of usage, techniques and styles, we take you on a journey through history, giving reason and insight as well as inspiration.

We can trace table arrangements back to Mesopotamia, the kingdom between Euphrates and Tigris some 6,000 years ago. There, priests and kings enjoyed garlands and wreaths, the two oldest known works of our profession, made by their skilled gardeners/florists. From wall paintings and murals we can see how richly their feasts were decorated.

From Egypt we have more evidence of the importance of flowers as decoration and techniques and actual materials used. Evidence from paintings as well as dried preserved flower works, over 4,000 years old, showing the strong colours used. Flowers used were chrysanthemum (Chrysanthemum), olive (Olea), roses (Rosa), poppies (Papaver), larkspur (Delphinium), cornflower (Centauries) and most important of all, the water lily (Nymphaea). An interesting fact is that fruits and vegetables were used in the works as well; this is seen in the garlands arranged on dinner tables. Feasts were garlanded on walls, the ceiling, around carafes and plates, wreaths and petals on table tops, guests being dressed in wreaths while giving the host bouquets.

Flowers were used whole or separated into petals arranged together for a mix of colours or used strictly according to religious importance of each flower. They tied or wove flower stems, using Papyrus fibres. Most elaborate of all being ones sewed together! Starting with a horizontal string, then one after the other, petal or flower head in between a leaf folded over the string and sewed together.

This use of garlands and wreaths made from flowers, herbs, greenery and fruits was also common in Greece, where each god had their own flower. This explains our use of some of those today! Most important when decorating tables were: goddess of love Aphrodite had white and red roses (Rosa), the god of fertility, wine and celebra-

Garland

tion Dionysus, wine and ivy (Hedera) leafs, the god of poetry and music, Apollo, had laurel (Laurus nobilis) leafs, the god of matrimony Hymenaios had myrtle (Myrthus), the goddess and protector of the city Athens, Athena, had violets (Viola). Wreaths and garlands were made of flowers such as roses and violets, including foliage, or only foliage were first mainly used to decorate temples, statues of gods, as offerings. Later when flowers were commonly cultivated and with new flowers and traditions brought from Persia by Alexander the Great, people started decorating their homes and especially dinner tables with garlands and wreaths.

In Rome they followed Greek traditions, continuing and improving techniques, but as with so many other things, they over did it to extremes. The rose (Rosa) was the flower. A party was not possible without roses, stuffed in cushions, as garlands on walls, between pillars, wreaths on carafes and tables, often made using individual petals piled on top of each other on strings, layers of petals thick as carpets on floors and even raining down on guests. There are stories of people drowning in rose rains, because of the Roses or the Rose spiced wine we do not know! The red carpet as we know it today is a version of the red rose covered streets for Caesar to walk upon. The use of flowers was excessive and what was not grown in Italy was brought in fortnightly from Egypt with the Alexandrian fleet. Besides the rose, other flowers e.g. lilies (Lilium), anemone (Anemone), daffodils (Narcissus), stock (Matthiola), all different herbs were used both for their good scents and colours. Wreaths were made on bases of thicker strings or plaits and then flowers and foliage tied and sometimes sewed around or elegantly sewed/piled, petal by petal on top of each other like pearls on a string! Garlands were either made in the same manner, free hanging or made with only a front on a base made from packed hay and grass for use on walls and doors. Romans believed in the curative powers of plants as well as their spiritual power, making wreaths from different herbs for their doors to protect the home from bad spirits. Most famous of them all was the one made from Hedera that was claimed to cure hangovers!

Rain of rose petals in Roman times

The Middle Ages, the battle of the flowers! With Christianity many traditions were abolished as pagan, but flowers were unstoppable. Unable to ban flower usage, the church changed and made flowers their own. Flowers symbolism and even their names were changed to suit the Christian message - flower use was christened! The rose, the 'symbol' of Rome became the most important symbol for the church, the white for Virgin Mary and the red for Christ. During most of the Middle Ages, flower use decreased because of wars, disease and poverty; but traditions were maintained by monasteries and the church. In royal courts and amongst the rich, fortunes were still spent on staging parties and dinners with magnificent table decorations, garlands and wreaths hanging from ceilings, on walls and on table sides. It was common to use flower petals on the floor with their good scents covering up less delicate ones. The profession was under pressure but at the end of the period flowers and flower works were once again sold at markets and professionals gathered in guilds, like the Chapelier des fleurs in Paris, but much reduced from Roman times.

Medieval centrepiece

The Renaissance brought the rebirth of science, humanities and arts in general, focusing now on earth, not heaven, with flowers once again flourishing.
There are many descriptions of huge Renaissance dinner parties, with everything but the flowers well described. We simply have to presume they used plenty of flowers. From the evidence we have we know decorations were getting more and more elaborate; miniature gardens complete with hedges, flower fields, fountains and statues, complemented with wreaths, garlands and flower petals. The most fascinating features are mentioned, such as the winter garden arrangement that slowly melts into spring and blooming summer through the course of dinner! Petals on tables being forerunners to our stitched and printed tablecloths. Technical help was packed moss, earth and often clay in which flowers and foliage were arranged. Decorating with flowers became more common in poorer homes because of new ways of furnishing homes with tables and cabinets. Often a vase with single flowers or a vase arrangement, brought nature to the tables of city homes. Flowers commonly used were all kinds of bulb flowers, garden and wild flowers, herbs and the ever present rose, most arranged in bright contrasting colours in the fashionable system of three colours, Triadic.

Renaissance centrepiece

With the discovery of new continents during the 1600s and early 1700s we got lots of new flowers into Europe, making botanics fashionable and creating trends in flowers. Passionate trends rage in trendsetting colonial countries such as France, Belgium, Holland and England. New Chinese roses (Rosa), peonies (Paeonia), orchids from South America, bulbs like fritillaries (Fritillaria), Hyacinths (Hyacinthus) from Middle Asia; bubbles like "Tulip mania" where tulips became speculative investments.

During the Baroque period, the "masculine" pompous and dark, the style was rich in materials and colours, with the purpose of showing wealth, often using accessories like new tropical fruits, exotic birds, butterflies and other rare objects. These were, of course, only for the richest in society.

Table arrangements and interior designs in general were extravagant, mixed arrangements of colourful flowers, combined with an extensive use of garlands and wreaths for celebrations and parties amongst royalty and nobles. This we know from popular paintings of flowers from the time. These "flower-paintings" from well-known artists like Ambrosius Bosschaert and Johann Knapp amongst many Dutch, Belgian and German painters were very fashionable. Mixing seasons as well as continents, these pictures didn't really accurately copy actual flower arrangements, but still they give a good idea of them!

Techniques used were several; some simply filled a vase or any container with flowers and greenery until full and stable. Another used soaked moss packed lightly into the container and pushed flowers into it for stability before adding water. When placing thicker stems they, on many occasions, used a stick of some kind to pre-pierce the moss for easier access. A third technique was to use branches, placed vertically into the container and then push flower steams in between these, creating a stable arrangement. Apart from these, they also used sand and clay as a holding medium for table arrangements with no water at all.
Table arrangements in these times were all more or less "arranged" and the expression, the look, gave the name, not the technique.

Ceiling decoration from the 1800s

During the Rococo, the more "feminine", graceful and brighter of the two, trends were once again set by the royal courts, especially the French. Where the longing for nature made them turn their great rooms into actual natural landscapes for parties. Nothing was impossible decorating these events but still the wreath and the garlands are the most common flower works, complimented by newer decorations. Popular were table decorations consisting of a centrepiece and garlands trailing out from that in the shapes of Cs and Ss.

Arrangements were done 'Baroque' style with new twists like the so called "vase in vase" arrangements where different sized containers were placed inside each other, like with a box in a box system. Flowers were placed into the spaces between containers and, by adding water, you have a fantastic arrangement! This was especially suitable for the flowers in fashion, elegant, fragile and often thin stemmed ones. A wide range of flowers were used – roses (Rosa), spray roses, carnations (Dianthus), myrtle (Myrthus), sweet pea (Lathyrus), columbines (Aquilegia), Freesias (Freesia), Lilacs (Syringa), Hyacinths (Hyacinthus) and other smaller natural blooms, loved for their scents and more feminine look.

If you could not afford real flowers, artificial ones were made of paper or fabric, a hobby for many women, rich and poor. This was a time when everything was decorated with flowers, fresh or fake!

Rococo table setting

During the first half of the 1800s, during the Empire period and mass industrialization, flower handicraft took big steps forward. Most major cities in Europe had flower markets and we see the first flower shops opening. Flowers were, before then, sold predominantly on markets. The first known flower shop was opened in Paris by a Madame Prevost. She and her two employees became famous for their bouquets and arrangements. Both bouquets and arrangements were made from individually wired flowers, all mixed to order. The next really big trend in flower arranging was the Biedermeier; a round domed or a slightly cone-shaped arrangement where the flowers are arranged in circles. This design started in Germany under the Biedermeier époque, spread over Europe and was later named after that same époque. All materials, flowers and greenery were wired, then, starting in the centre and working outwards, creating one circle after the other, stems parallel or totally random. These Biedermeier arrangements were made in all sizes and fashions and were complemented with garlands in between the candelabra connecting the centrepieces, on table sides and table cloths.

Rococo table garland

Table setting from the 1800s

In the latter part of the 1800s, Romantic period decorations become more popular and get a more natural and open look inspired by gardens and nature. Flowers loosely arranged in vases, pots and pitchers preferably picked from your garden became high fashion, especially in Victorian England. Decorations were made in pots, containers and the increasingly popular basket, arranged in moss for water supply and stability. Flowers were all wired like bouquet designs of that time, making it possible for the florist to create angles and special shapes.

Table setting from the early 1900s

At the turn of the century to the 1900s, we see rapid development of the profession and new flower shops opening to cater to the demands of the growing cities.
The further away from nature people got and the richer they became, the bigger the need for flowers. A wider selection with better quality was available through better growing techniques and imports from the Riviera. We see proper education for florists starting, exhibitions and competitions all to strengthen and develop the profession.

Arrangements in general were getting bigger and more impressive and, as mentioned above, moss, hay, branches and wires were the materials used, giving all florists at the time black fingers, not green ones! When using baskets and the especially well known Elisa basket they were either lined with waxed waterproof paper or customized metal containers were fitted inside, and then the preferred medium was inserted and soaked.
The expression a la mode is the Nature-inspired Jugend/Art Nouveau style giving us arrangements with lots of garden and "wild" flowers like peonies, phlox, garden roses, various grasses and foliage in open cone shapes. Another common form was the Pyramid, more open than the latter one and obviously shaped like a pyramid. Arrangements stayed rather decorative, nature inspired with a wide variety of flowers

in the same composition or with more classic materials, often using one single flower type, like roses or carnations, with foliage. Flowers were arranged in all available containers, each household using and showing their most precious bowls, jardinières, and exclusive china with flowers matching them. Low arrangements with foliage trailing over tablecloths and interconnecting with other arrangements, several to a table, light delicate garlands. Taller ones were made in vases, jardinières, and special flower holders, a metal stand some 50-70 cm tall with a wider glass bowl on the top, generously decorated with flowers and e.g. Plumose (Asparagus), ivy (Hedera) cascading down towards the table top. These arrangements were mostly accompanied with candelabras, figurines, fruit plates and other beautiful objects to create a rich and extravagant atmosphere.

Even though the revolutionary flower medium, flower foam, the first being Oasis, saw the light of day in 1956 it only changed the technique of arrangements. Design and expression stayed the same; decorative style was still predominant until the late 1960s and early 1970s. Other alternative materials and holders are now also being introduced mainly from USA. Glass globes with holes into them for flower stems, plastic holders of many designs to be placed into vases or containers for arranging. Most common was the Fakir-bed originating from Japan, put in vases and most commonly low plates and bowls making flower arranging something for everyone, not only the florist! These led to new designs and styles!

Several structures for arranging table settings
(plastic, glass, metal, lead and fakir bed)

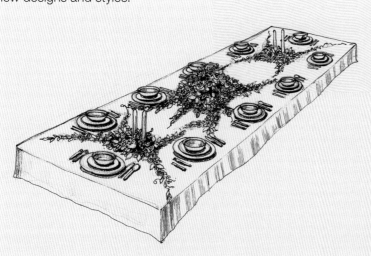

20th century table setting

For most of history we have seen variations of the Decorative style, but from the 70s we see a rapid change with the introduction of the Formal linear and Vegetative styles. Overall we can say that arrangements got more attention, inspiration and skill put into them and the full potential of flower foam was used in expressing these new styles, simply because it made them possible.

Formal linear is, as the name itself indicates, all about forms of blooms and foliage and lines of stems and branches, where the search for contrasts is crucial. Contrasts in materials, textures and, most significantly, in colours, make this style totally different to the decorative. Here each single material is important, compared to the Decorative style where the volume and total expression is important. This was inspired by Japan and their Ikebana style.

The Vegetative style is once again something totally different, taking inspiration from nature, habitats, seasons and ways of growing. Here we see small landscapes or the essence of a special season or habitat!
What we see in the 80s and 90s is the use of more twigs, branches and other botanical and artificial materials, leading into our next new style, the Transparent style. Designs where the use of stems and lines are as important as flower heads. These works, in overlapping designs, creating transparent volumes, falling, cascading, rising, moving in one or several directions have become fashionable amongst florists.

Recently, arrangement designs have become more and more personal and individual, often mixing styles and with a more varied use of accessory materials giving focus to expression instead of style. In floristry, as in society, we are looking for personal expression.
Looking back through history we see how the use of flowers has changed according to historical époques and availability to a constantly wider audience. Like most trends in society, changes moved slowly up until the early 20th century when things speeded up with constant change to our time now, reflecting the tempo of modern life. We see how technique is the core of arranging and when we got more and easier materials to use arrangements became commercially affordable for everyone. Styles and shapes are reused in many ways. Working with flowers, petals and greenery spread out directly on tablecloths, Roman-style; we use fruits and vegetables mixed with flowers and lately we see flowers arranged in more expressive and unique containers like a century ago. We can now match design, style and technical features for a themed table setting and maybe most importantly of all we can use appropriate techniques for each design, much better than foam to met the demands of today's environmentally conscious society.
With knowledge and inspiration from history and with today's fantastic selection and quality of flowers and new materials, the challenge for the designer is to show his or her talent and imagination as well as to express the message the client wants to convey with the arrangement. To show the possibilities of decorating tables with flowers, making it as important as it once was and making it the natural norm for any dinner. We will achieve this by matching the right techniques, materials, containers and flowers to create a table arrangement with a strong personal emotional expression!

The future of the table arrangement

Table arrangements of various kinds have always been with us, from a simple flower on the table, to bigger decorations or themed artistic pieces. Table decorations strengthen the atmosphere with their colours, scents and the unique expressions of each single bloom.

Here we see a chance for the future. People don't always know all possibilities and effects of floral arrangements. We need to show them the creative opportunities for using flowers on the dinner table, customizing them for each meal depending on the meaning of the gathering – romantic, professional or social. Working towards a more personal touch, either reflecting the customer, receiver or florist. Use new designs, shapes, colour combinations, techniques and most important of all, introduce new materials into the designs!

Florists have to lead trends all the time. Look at flowers and discover the differences in their personalities. Let flowers express themselves or use them to reflect personalities and emotions. Use their full potential. Today and even more so in the future, alternative materials to foam are emerging, for aesthetic-creative as well as environmental reasons.

Emotion and functionality need to be combined with good skills and knowledge about our products to compete with other skills and decorations for the dinner table. When it was, in the past, enough just to make a centre piece for the table we now need to set a higher standard and show that we can translate the wishes of our clients and work beyond those in realization of the designs.

Here we talk about helping and advising the client with the whole concept of the dinner. How to pair flowers and food, the origin of it and the expression in texture and colours. The overall theme of the dinner which can be everything from cozy to intimate, classic, modern, rococo, Indian, Japanese… and has to be expressed in flowers, flower characters, personality, colour, shapes, scents, botanical as well as artificial materials, and the techniques we use for mechanical and esthetical expression. All of this put together will give results far beyond anyone's expectations!

Be it a smaller gathering with friends, a bigger dinner party, a birthday celebration or a big commercial event, it is important to theme and put energy in the table setting. Not only something beautiful but something with other aspects of design that attract attention and create discussions around the table. No occasion or budget is too small or too big for our creativity.

In short, inspiration is nothing we are short of; we simply need to translate and theme it into the needs and desires of our clients. Remembering the historic and classical ways of working; matching that with today's circumstances and materials and new needs of environmentally friendly aspects thus creating table arrangements of the future.

The future is alive with design concepts, themeing the whole table setting, personalized and customized table arrangements for each and every occasion combined with the ever present and important emotional aspect of the occasion!

Step by step

Curvy Spring

Designer
Tomas
Materials
Betula (bark) / birch bark
Calamus rotang / pulp cane
Hyacinthus orientalis / Eastern hyacinth
Salix / willow
Syringa vulgaris / lilac
Tulipa / tulip
Viburnum opulus / Guelder rose
elastic bands
firm cardboard
glass tubes
metal wire 0.7
ornamental twine
tape

Design This elongated design optically extends the table. As it weaves its way through the table settings, it creates unity and connection among the dinner guests. Thanks to the choice of materials and the fresh green colour, the arrangement brings a cheerful spring feeling to the table.
Technique Just as everything in the human body is supported by the spine, everything in this design is suspended from a piece of cardboard. It determines the design's basic shape and holds together all accessories, including tubes, flowers and Salix twigs. The glass tubes are attached to the cardboard with elastic bands. A very simple and aesthetic way of working.
Emotions It is as if a piece of nature is walking across our table. This arrangement immediately puts us in a natural spring mood where dinner guests and nature become one. Spring at its finest!

1 A sturdy basis is crucial for this arrangement. Cut a strip of firm cardboard that does not crease. The length of the strip is determined by the length of the table; the height is 5 cm less than that of the glass tubes. Reinforce the cardboard strip by taping a few metal wires along it; this will also help you bend the cardboard in the desired shape at the end. Finally cover the cardboard in Betula bark.

2 Cover the strip with wide natural pulp cane. To prevent the pulp cane from cracking or breaking, first immerse it in boiling water. Repeat the same with finer, coloured pulp cane to place the odd accent here and there. Then bend the strip in the desired shape. The glass tubes are attached by means of elastic bands. The *Salix* twigs are strapped across the cardboard. Make sure all glass tubes and twigs are level and touch the surface.

3 Now arrange the flowers: start with the dominant Lilac, and distribute them evenly across the strip of cardboard.

4 Finish off by distributing the other flowers across the arrangement. Do not place and combine flowers in the tubes together with the hyacinths, as these give off an oil which is harmful to other flowers.

17

Vitamines

Designer
Per
Materials
Acacia floribunda / Gossamer wattle
Citrus sinensis (fruit) / orange
Craspedia globosa / golden drumstick
Gloriosa rothschildiana / glory lily
Phormium / New Zealand flax
Sandersonia aurantiaca / Chinese lantern lily
coloured wooden skewers
Mizuhiki wire
pearl-headed pins
thin translucent plastic (different colours)

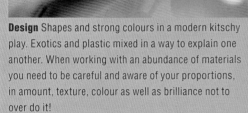

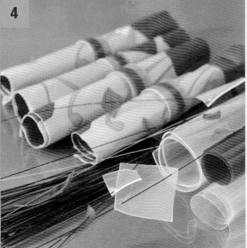

Design Shapes and strong colours in a modern kitschy play. Exotics and plastic mixed in a way to explain one another. When working with an abundance of materials you need to be careful and aware of your proportions, in amount, texture, colour as well as brilliance not to over do it!

Technique Regular arranging technique but instead of foam we use oranges. This is a well tested technique and orange juice works fine as substitute for foam and water, keeping the flowers fresh for some 2 days, more than enough for a table arrangement!

Emotion Strong colours, shapes and textures all blended into a strong yet harmonic expression. A conversation piece of true magnitude! This will awake emotions and discussions during dinner, being something new and different in all aspects.

1 Strong warm colours are the focus of this arrangement. Remove the foliage from all flowers and stems and cut away the green tops of both Mimosa and Sandersonia. It is important to start with well-watered, fresh and strong materials.

2 Start by placing the oranges on the table in a pattern of your liking and connect them with coloured wooden skewers. Make sure to place the skewers in the mid to upper part of the fruits not to lose too much fruit juice.

3 Finalize the outer line of the main rectangular shape by creating a crossed pattern with the Craspedias in between and over the oranges.

4 To add brilliance and a kitschy feel to the table setting cut thin translucent plastic in pieces. Put them on Mizuhiki wires to decorate the arrangement and use the remaining parts to make napkin rings for your table setting.

5 For the actual floral part, continue the crossed pattern and overlap the materials. Make sure everything is well cut. Pre-pierce the oranges with a sharp thick pin when needed. Remember to push the stems deeply into the oranges for optimal liquid support.

19

Fusion

Designer
Max
Materials
Betula / Birch
Iris
Jasminum polyanthum / Jasmine
Muscari / Grape hyacinth
Ranunculus / Turban buttercup
Tulipa / Tulip
eggs
glue gun
tea light candles

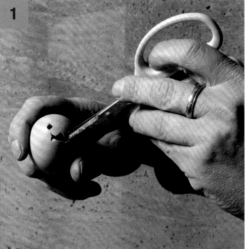

Design A design with many spring elements: eggs that serve as water carriers, and spring flowers in their cheerful colours. The sumptuous look of this table decoration intensifies the spring feeling!

Technique The egg shells, that serve as little vases, are glued together in the shape of a table. The basic structure of *Jasminum* and *Betula* is there to support the heavier flowers. Make sure there is enough depth and prevent squared and parallel lines.

Emotions A rich, colourful table decoration that boasts all the elements of spring. Positive and brimming with life. An excellent start to a new summer season!

1 Blow out the eggs, carefully pierce little holes in the shell and tap a piece away with some scissors. Clean the egg shells inside, which will hold the water for the flowers.

2 Carefully glue the egg shells together but leave some room for tea light candles which will be placed in amongst the egg shells in due course. Scatter the egg shells across the entire table, except for where the plates and cutlery will be and make sure there is enough room for the dinner guests to have their meal in comfort!

21

Fusion

3 Place the tea light candles in the empty spaces. Carefully fill the egg shells with water. Do not overfill them as the flowers need to be inserted yet and we do not want any water spilling.

4 With the Jasminum, create a natural structure. Not only does this make for an interesting pattern, this construction can also support heavier flowers. Do the same with the Betula, but examine its direction of growth to create a natural look.

5 The flowers can now be inserted. Start with the heaviest flowers (tulips) and create an attractive pattern. Make sure there is enough depth and that the colour scheme is attractive. By way of finishing touch, attach a Betula to the napkins with a ribbon to marry everything together.

Tulips gone Wild

Designer
Per
Materials
Tulipa / tulip
Xerophyllum tenax / bear grass
bullion wire
floral fix
glass candle holders
metal angel hair
Mizuhiki wire
spool wire

1 Select the most beautiful botanical tulips. To create harmony in your arrangement, select some colour tones from the flowers when choosing the colours of the binding wire. Clear all tulips of their bigger leaves to show more of the elegant stems. Clean all dirt from the bear grass to emphasise the green colour spectrum at their bases.

2 Use the candle holders as a base to create the structures by applying two strips of floral fix onto them. Add the well-dried bear grass bit by bit and fix it in the desired position by circling the base with spool wire.

3 Mix some Mizuhiki wires in between the bear grass all around the base for stability and flexibility reasons. As shown on the photo, you can bend all of the bear grass strings in one way or split the bundle in two halves that can be bent in two opposite directions.

4 Cover the base with metal angel hair and secure it with bullion wire of the same colour. Curve and rotate the grass and use the same materials as in the base, to create the top of each structure. The tulips can then easily be placed inside the water-filled structure.

Design Formal linear and decorative at the same time! This way of working emphasizes the character and personality of one single flower, the botanic tulip; its curves, its joyful and almost childlike appearance and its pale, shy colours.

Technique Wiring and arranging techniques used both for practical and decorative reasons. Even some weaving technique can be applied to get the flowers where you want using the bear grass structure. When put in water, the structure can easily be maintained for a long time when not in use on the table.

Emotions Movement and freedom! The tulips will curve in any direction they like, no matter what we want. Be smart in allowing this and making good use of it. If you can't beat them, join them!

25

Mysticism

Designer
Tomas

Materials
Phalaenopsis / Moth orchid
Tillandsia xerographica
2 shiny boards (black and white)
cotton balls
glue gun
white and black Christmas baubles
white beads

1 Carefully select the different Christmas baubles and distribute them across the two boards. Size and colour are paramount here. We draw an imaginary semi-circle on the boards on which we attach the baubles with hot glue. This creates an attractive and fascinating design.

2 To connect the separate baubles optically and create movement, we use Tillandsia. Create a fluid line, so that an attractive S-shape comes about that flows from one board onto the next. In this way, one harmonious centrepiece is created instead of two separate boards.

3 Pour water into the Christmas baubles so that the Phalaenopsis is not dry when preparing the arrangement. Here too, respect the flowing line and allow the flower heads to point in every direction so that all dinner guests can fully enjoy the flowers.

Design The contrast between black and white is the most striking feature in this design. The two shiny boards instantly create a sense of rigidity, which is broken, however, not only by the elegance of the flowers, but also by the way in which they are placed among the Christmas baubles.
Technique We provide a water reservoir for the flowers by attaching the Christmas baubles with hot glue onto the boards. The baubles are neatly linked by the Tillandsia. For an extra festive touch, shiny black twigs are woven through the flowers.
Emotions Yin and Yang. Black and white. Male and female. A fusion of Western and Eastern styles and influences evokes a contrasting emotion. The black and white duality of the design transports us to a world of mysticism.

4 Finish off with black sticks, which add a festive touch but also accentuate the black and white contrast. The black berries at the end of the twigs are also perfect in this arrangement.

27

Happy X-Mas

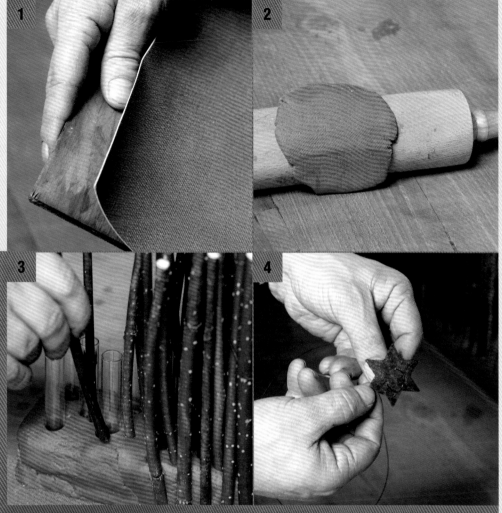

Designer
Max

Materials
Anigozanthos / Kangaroo paw
Anthurium andreanum / Flamingo flower
Cornus alba 'Sibirica' / Red-stemmed dogwood
Eucalyptus
Euphorbia fulgens / Scarlet plume
Hypericum / St John's Wort
Ranunculus / Turban buttercup
Syringa vulgaris / Lilac
Tulipa / Tulip
oasis (dry)
pine cones
plastic stars
plywood
red plasticine
red twine
red wallpaper
test tubes

1 Saw a piece of plywood that is 12 cm wide to match the length of the table. Cover with red wallpaper. Choose a red that is close to that of the Cornus. Cut the dry oasis into strips of 8 cm wide and 4 cm high and glue these to the centre of the plywood.

2 Roll out the plasticine thinly with a rolling pin and cut it into pieces that fit over the oasis exactly. Knead the plasticine and press it down sufficiently so that it is stuck to the oasis.

3 Cut the Cornus into pieces of approx. 20 cm and insert these deeply in the oasis in a parallel manner. Also insert the test tubes in the oasis at the same time.

4 Thread the stars and Hypericum berries on red twine. Smooth them out so that they bend down a little. Strip the leaves from the flowers, hold the Euphorbia under the tap for a moment to stem the bleeding. Insert the flowers in the test tubes, starting with the largest. Glue some pine cones in amongst the flowers. Make sure that the flower heads poke out from underneath the Cornus twigs. Finish off the arrangement with the threaded stars and Hypericum berries.

Design The colour red is paramount in this arrangement. The parallel Cornus twigs on the red-plasticine base, with the flowers, also in reds and browns, just above the twigs evoke a very warm and intense feeling.
Technique Apply the plasticine carefully. Make sure it sticks down and is not torn. Use enough test tubes to accommodate all the flowers.
Emotions The intense red colours give this creation a warm and powerful glow, which is intensified by the robust male shape and proportion.

Summertime

Designer
Per

Materials
Ammi visnaga / bishop's weed
Chrysanthemum frutescens / marguerite daisy
Malus (fruit) / apple
Panicum 'Fountain' / switch grass
Tanacetum parthenium / feverfew
Viburnum opulus / Guelder rose
apple corer
glass tubes
wallpaper
wooden plank

1 Start by selecting big and beautiful, spotless apples. For stability reasons, choose apples that are relatively flat at the bottom. Clean off the foliage of the flowers and grasses and cut them all at the same length.

2 Use an apple corer, but do not go all the way through the fruit. Stop at 2/3 depth and pull out the core with the seeds. Use a sharp tool to avoid flimsy brown edges.

3 Adjust your apple corer to a size matching the glass tubes as closely as possible. Holes that are too small won't work because the apples will break when forcing the tubes in. If the holes are too big, simply wrap some floral tape around the tubes to stabilize them.

4 Place the apples with the glass tubes directly on the table or put them on a wooden plank dressed in matching wallpaper. Arrange the flowers and grasses in an irregular rhythm; placement is only secondary to the decorative aspect.

Design Decoratively arranged table piece with the feel of a sunlit summer field, a fresh breeze blowing through, ideal for that relaxed gathering amongst friends. Refined simplicity at its best!
Technique Arrangement technique in glass tubes, like freely arranged flowers in vases. Think of the water supply for the flowers: use well-sized tubes or choose flowers that need little water. Use a pipette to refill the tubes. Keep the apples cool and spray them to prevent oxidation around the hole of the glass tube.
Emotions A summer's day spent walking in flowering fields on the countryside, thinking of lunch with friends, or spending the afternoon reading a book in your hammock. My summer's dream!

Woody tenderness

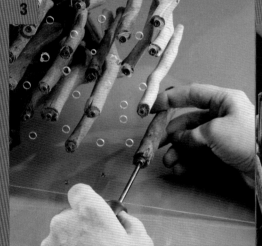

Designer
Tomas
Materials
Adiantum raddianum/ maidenhair fern
Fritillaria meleagris / snake's head fritillary
Myosotis / forget-me-not
Ranunculus asiaticus / turban buttercup
acrylic sheet
driftwood

1 A waterproof dish, an acrylic sheet and driftwood form the main ingredients of this arrangement. The flowers are selected based on colour and character. The acrylic sheet must have a minimum thickness of 0.5 cm and measure 120 by 25 cm. When the acrylic sheet extends beyond the dish, this will create a less compact, less plain feeling.

2 According to their function, drill holes of different diameters in the acrylic sheet. Use the smallest holes to attach the sheet to the driftwood, and the slightly bigger ones for the flower stalks. Since Ranunculus is used, the holes need to be slightly bigger. When drilling, make the holes gradually bigger to keep the acrylic sheet from cracking.

3 Attach the different sticks to the acrylic sheet. Screw them down carefully, so as not to crack the sheet.

4 When the dish has been filled with water, the flowers can be placed among the driftwood. The stalks remain in place thanks to the holes in the acrylic sheet, while the flower heads are supported by the wood. Place the larger flowers first and finish off with the more fragile Myosotis and Fritillaria.

Design A compact and heavy design that instantly fills up a table. The surprise element of this arrangement is that the acrylic sheet allows us a glimpse behind the scenes.
Technique The driftwood supports the flowers and keeps them in place. This natural support base makes the use of oasis unnecessary. The holes in the acrylic sheet can hold the sticks, as well as the flower stalks, and the flowers can easily access the water. This way of working is not only functional but is also decorative and gives the arrangement a more attractive shape.
Emotions We create a relaxed, lively atmosphere of a homely, yet intense gathering.

Discus

Designer
Per
Materials
Chrysanthemum 'Yoko Ono' / Chrysanthemum
Diospyros lotus (fruit) / Date plum
Gypsophila paniculata / Gypsophila
Helleborus argutifolius / Corsican hellebore
Hypericum / St John's Wort
Viburnum opulus 'Roseum' / Snowball tree
2 dishes
cabbage leaves
cold glue
lettuce types
oasis
spray glue

Design Design in which only curves are used that are ever recurring. A strong, calm base of Gypsophila forms a striking contrast with the green flowers and makes for a strong and unexpected arrangement. The plate decoration with green cabbage leaves reinforces the effect.
Technique Two techniques are mixed here: gluing and inserting. If you only have a shallow dish, you can also cover the entire dish with oasis. Do make sure that the arrangement retains its rigid look.
Emotion Rigid, fresh and businesslike, yet relaxing, original and tasteful. An arrangement that can be used for many occasions.

Discus

1 Fill the dishes with oasis, to just under the rim of the dish's outside edge and a little deeper in the centre. Use cold glue to glue to the sides and pack with Gypsophila. Please note that Gypsophila can only be used in one direction.

2 Also fill the centre of the dish. Do this very compactly and use small bundles of Gypsophila. The dish is hollowed out towards the centre. Keep a circular recess on one side. Make sure both dishes are identical.

3 Trim the edges to achieve a rigid and neat look. Repair the less attractive sections with the remainder of the Gypsophila flowers.

4 Now fill in the circular recesses with flowers. Do this level with the Gypsophila. Decorate the plates with cabbage leaves and fill them with rocket.

Passion!

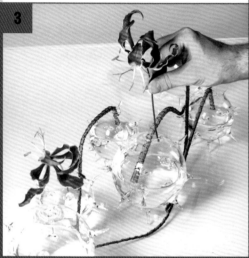

Designer
Tomas

Materials
Gloriosa rotschildiana / glory lily
Lathyrus odoratus / sweet pea
Mandevilla 'Sunmanderemi' (Sundaville)
Ranunculus asiaticus / buttercup
Xerophyllum tenax / bear grass
red winding wire
vases (in two different sizes)

1 The choice of vases and their positioning is of the utmost importance in this table setting. Position them in a straight line and respect their different heights. In this way some three dimensionality can be added to the table and the flowers can flow in a playful manner from one vase to another.

2 We wrap the bear grass with red winding wire, referring to the colour of the flowers and fiery passion. Use plenty of wire, to make manipulating the bundles easier and to ensure they keep their curve once bent into the desired shape.

3 Place the bundles of bear grass in the vases and create an interesting interplay of lines. Put three large vases aside to use them as bowls for the fish later on. When arranging the flowers it is best to start with the dominant Ranunculus, providing the resting points and the rhythm in the setting. Continue with the long elegant Gloriosa, let them float naturally and spontaneously in between the different vases. The gracious Mandevilla tendrils connect the different vases. Add a dash of female grace with the fragile Lathyrus.

4 As a finishing touch we add the fish to the water. Take care of the well-being of the fish, make sure the water has the correct temperature and provide the fish with enough water by putting them in the biggest containers. Plants, animals and humans together at one table: a fantastic story!

Design Combining fauna and flora makes this table arrangement very attractive. The addition of small fish creates a playful touch and adds movement. The shape of the vases, combined with the fiery red colour of the flowers add to the idea of passion and temperament. The big red Ranunculus provide resting points for the eyes, while the other flowers give the arrangement naturalness and flow.
Technique The positioning of the vases is very important in this table setting. The different sized vases are connected optically by the bear grass wrapped in red thread. At the same time these bear grass bundles create the feel of movement that is so vital in the setting.
Emotions The combination of vases, fish and flowers make up for a harmonious result. The crimson red, the movement, the texture of the containers and the well proportioned flowers only make for a more passionate result.

Silence

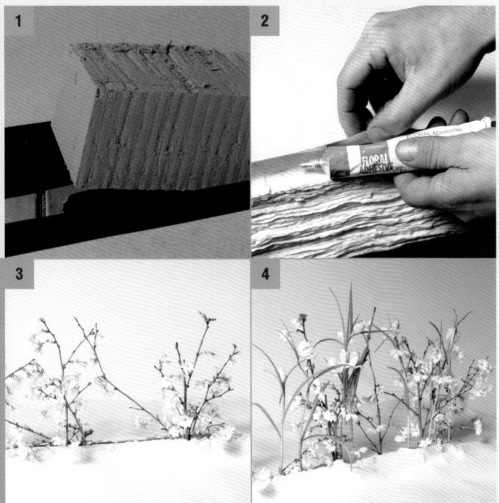

Designer
Max
Materials
Fritillaria meleagris / Snake's head fritillary
Helleborus 'Christmas Glory'
Muscari / Grape hyacinth
Prunus
asian paper
cold glue
oasis
plywood
white rice

1 Make a table top of plywood, 6 cm tick, with a groove across the entire length of 5 cm wide. Fill this groove with oasis that is first covered in plastic.

2 Tear the paper in narrow, equal bands and glue them to the side of the table top. The easiest way is to fold down the sticky side. This will also add stability and provide a better cover. Glue three whole sheets of Asian paper on top.

3 Moisten the paper above the oasis and carefully rip it open. The result should not be straight or neat but should appear ripped open. First of all, insert the Prunus in the oasis, as this ensures that the paper remains open.

4 Now add the Fritillaria. Rinse the Muscari bulbs well and insert them into the oasis by using metal wire. Finish off the oasis with white grains of rice.

Design The design is based on the contrast between soft and strong. The soft paper is ripped open by the growing force of the flowers and also blends in perfectly with them.

Technique Place the paper on a smaller table – this offers interesting possibilities. When the paper is moist, it is easier to rip it. First fold over the glued rim.

Emotion The soft natural materials in shades of white create a sense of purity and relaxation. Still and strikingly powerful, despite the extremely fragile flowers!

Parallel!

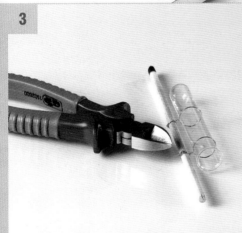

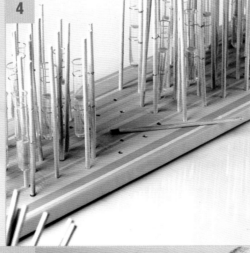

Designer
Tomas

Materials
Allium neapolitanum / Italian garlic
Ammi visnaga / toothpick weed
Cucumis dipsaceus / wild cucumber
Dianthus 'Green Trick' / dianthus
Lathyrus odoratus / sweet pea
Muscari armenicum / grape hyacinth
board
glass tubes
plant sticks
plastic wallpaper
silver-coloured thread
spray paint (white)

1 The basis for this arrangement is a sturdy, smooth board with a minimum thickness of 1.5 cm. The length of the board should be in proportion to the length of the table. Bear in mind that there should be sufficient space on the table for the plates and cutlery and that the dinner guests should not be hindered by it in any way. When drilling holes, use a bit that has the same diameter as the sticks.

2 Sand down all holes and rough patches and place the sticks in the appropriate holes. At the same time the sticks can be sprayed white. Remove the sticks when dry. Then, cover the board in self-adhesive and water-resistant wallpaper. Start in the centre and work your way outwards to avoid creasing and bubbling under the paper.

3 Tie glass tubes to half of the painted sticks. Tie them in two places to avoid them toppling over when flowers are placed in them. Use white or silver-coloured twine.

4 Pierce the paper where the holes are – these can be felt by running your finger over them – and twist the sticks into them so that everything looks nicely rigid and harmonious. Distribute the glass tubes evenly across the board.

Design A board, plastic wallpaper and plant sticks are the main ingredients of this design. This rigid and elongated design appears as male and dominant on the table. This is balanced out, though, by the choice of colour of the flowers and the paper, which provide a softer, feminine counterweight.
Technique By placing the sticks in the board, a base is created for our flowers. Stick down the wallpaper very tautly. The sticks are not only decorative, they are also used to support the glass tubes.
Emotions A first communion is always a very special occasion. The table is generously decorated with flowers for the party girl or boy. This colourful arrangement manages to give a modern twist to this traditional event and reflects the beauty of the day.

5 Finish off with flowers. Distribute them evenly across the arrangement to obtain a harmonious look.

43

Autumn's gold

Designer
Per
Materials
Acer campestre / field maple
Gloriosa rothschildiana / glory lily
Malus (fruit) / apple
Rosa (fruit) / rose bottle
glass tubes
glue and hot glue gun
metal stick
spray glue

1 For this arrangement you can use all the wonderful materials you can gather during a walk on a warm autumn's day. Look for colours that harmonize with the wonderful Gloriosas.

2 I use Acer leaves for their beautiful colour spectrum, their size and excellent durability. Select the most beautiful ones and pierce them onto a metal stick. Simply spray glue on some leaves to cover the metal stick at both ends.

3 Use a hot glue gun to add the glass tubes to the structure, making sure that the tubes do not exceed the height of the leaves. Use plenty of glue all along the glass tubes for security.

4 Place the glass tubes in between the leaves, wherever you want to place the flowers later on. Arrange the glass tubes in an irregular rhythm, bearing in mind the size and volume of water needed by each flower.

5 Once all tubes are filled with water, arrange the flowers in a decorative and even way. Make use of the stems of the leaves to secure and direct the flowers. Spray with water to keep fresh longer.

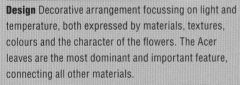

Design Decorative arrangement focussing on light and temperature, both expressed by materials, textures, colours and the character of the flowers. The Acer leaves are the most dominant and important feature, connecting all other materials.
Technique A mix of arranging, piercing and gluing techniques is used in this table arrangement. Adjust the tube sizes according to the water need of the chosen flowers. Kept cold and sprayed with water the structure can last quite some time.
Emotions Autumn, the time of the year to slow down, relax and remember, a time to contemplate during long walks in nature, lit in the most fantastic colours. Autumn is my favourite time of the year: the scents, the sound of rustling leaves, the sun playing in the trees and the biting cold!

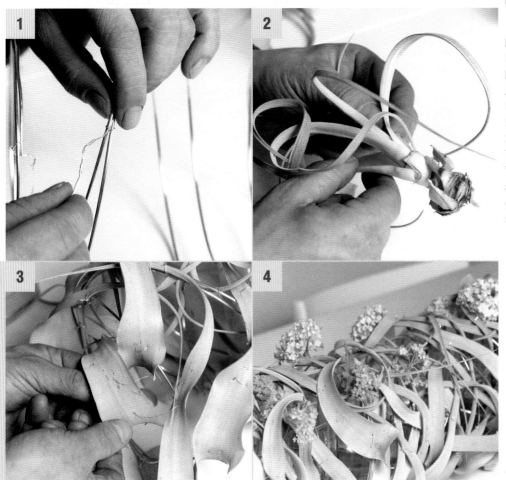

Serene

Designer
Max
Materials
Anemone coronaria
Hyacinthus / hyacinth
Ranunculus / Turban buttercup
Syringa vulgaris / Lilac
Tillandsia xerographica
Viburnum opulus 'Roseum' / Snowball tree
aluminium wire (2mm)
glass vases
silver twine

1 Make four loops of aluminium wire of approx 20-25 cm diameter and tie these together cross-wise with twine. Make sure all points of contact are tied together well so as to create a sturdy frame.

2 Peel the Tillandsia xerographica and cut away any wilting sections.

3 With twine, tie the Tillandsia from the bottom up. Try to interlace as much as possible. Heed the direction of the leaf from the bottom up (see photograph). Do not completely close off the top, as the flowers need to be placed in them.

4 Fill up the snake with vases filled with water and start inserting the flowers. Defoliate beforehand and cut off the Viburnum. Do keep a piece of twig at the bottom of the latter so as to stop the stalk from drooping. Now place the flowers in amongst the Tillandsia leaves.

Design The Tillandsia snake creates natural movement. Colour and use of material turn this arrangement into a serene and attractive piece.
Technique A base of twine, fleshed out with a transparent Tillandsia piece, interlaced as much as possible and knotted where necessary. The flowers in the glass vases that are filled with water are easy to insert in amongst the Tillandsia.
Emotion The colours and use of materials evoke the restrained, yet fresh sense of a new start. This design is therefore ideal for a wedding, for example.

47

Summary of a happy year

1 **2**

3 **4**

Designer
Tomas
Materials
Adiantum raddianum / Maidenhair fern
Phalaenopsis (mini) / Moth orchid (mini)
Saintpaulia / African violet
cotton balls
glass tubes
paper (A4)
wallpaper paste

1 Start by ripping strips of A4 paper. Opt for paper with a bluish tinge for extra effect. Make the strips about 5 cm high. Create a coarser look by ripping the top edge roughly and unevenly.

2 Glue the separate paper strips with wallpaper paste. Start from the centre. Make sure the strips are not stuck together completely, but leave a sufficient gap between the different paper layers. Only place paste on the outside of the strips.

3 To ensure that the glass tubes do not slip, glue these in place between the paper strips with cold glue. Distribute the tubes not across the full circle but across only half of it. Otherwise, the entire paper surface would be covered in flowers.

4 Distribute the Saintpaulia flowers across the design. Due to the delicate nature of these flowers, they all need to be placed in glass tubes, except for the orchids, which can be distributed across the surface with cold glue. Do make sure, though, that the orchid stalks are glued down properly, so that the flower can retain water for longer and thus stay fresh for longer. Finish off by scattering cotton balls over the table arrangement.

Design Here the paper claims all attention, which is why it is refined by giving it an uneven edge. The roughness of the torn paper forms a striking contrast with the softness of the flowers. We have not completely covered the design with flowers, because we want to let the attractive structure and texture of the paper dominate the design. The cotton balls add a playful and wintry touch.
Technique By winding paper and gluing it in place, a large circle is formed. By winding paper around it, and gluing this in place, a large circle is formed. The glass tubes are glued in between the paper layers.
Emotions The many circles carry the flowers. We are careering, as it were, from the old year into the new year which will hopefully be filled with memorable encounters and intense experiences.

49

Summery transparency

Designer
Max
Materials
Anthurium andreanum / Flamingo flower
Daucus
Eustoma russeliana
Gloriosa rothschildiana / Glory lily
Lupinus / lupine
Nerine bowdenii
Rosa / Rose
aluminium wire
plexiglas
test tubes

1 Drill two holes (2mm) into the Plexiglas. The distance between the holes is determined by the diameter of the test tubes. Fold the aluminium wire in half and insert the ends into the drilled holes. Twist the wire three times rigidly.

2 Do the same with the test tubes, but wind the wire around them first for a good connection with the Plexiglas.

3 Scatter the Plexiglas sheets and tubes randomly to create a more exciting arrangement, and fill up the tubes with water up to two fingers from the top.

4 Strip the flowers from their leaves and insert them into the tubes. The top of the flowers makes up about 1/ 3 of the entire height. For the sake of stability, and to add an element of quirkiness, do not place the tubes in a straight line.

Design In this design, vase, base and flowers become one, which makes for a very airy and transparent centrepiece.
Technique The base is made from transparent material and is attached with light thread. The flowers are arranged in the vases in a simple manner.
Emotion A sense of a carefree summer's day, casual, yet well thought-out, rich in colour, yet bleached by the sun, transparent, yet compact.

51

Circle of fire

Designer
Per
Materials
Dianthus / carnation
Gloriosa rothschildiana / glory lily
Ilex verticillata / common winterberry
Phormium / New Zealand flax
foam wreath
pearl-headed pins

1 Think about the colour division when choosing the carnations to get a good rhythm in the final design. Clean the Gloriosa from pollen and cut the Ilex in 10 cm pieces.

2 Start by covering the sides of the well-watered foam wreath with Phormium leaves. Work in two layers, starting from the bottom and ending the Phormium leaves some 2-3 cm above the surface of the foam. Secure with pearl-headed pins and use an abundance of additional pins for purely decorative purposes.

3 Arrange the carnations in two parallel circles in grouped colour lines overlapping one another to create a moving or circling expression. Place the flowers as deeply as possible, so they rest on the edge of the Phormium leaves.

4 Put the Gloriosa into the foam, arranging the flower heads mostly on the outside of the wreath, some on top and only a few on the inside. Place the pieces of pinned Ilex onto the carnations and use them to bend and put the Gloriosas in position and for decorative reasons.

5 Once all Gloriosas and Ilexes are placed in an irregular and quite strongly grouped pattern, leave some parts of the wreath bare and pin on the orchids as a finishing touch.

Design Decorative wreath in foam with the most simple and beautiful of flowers – the carnation – as a base providing colour and texture, and letting the other flowers shine and show off their pride and joy. All materials reflect the flaming red of fire!
Technique Arranging technique in foam as a base for the further work. Pinning is used for fixing the Phormium leaves around the outside of the wreath as well as for the flowers on the inside and the details on the top. Make sure the Gloriosa and orchids are well watered before using them.
Emotions Fire has a magical attraction, we are spellbound by looking into the flames... Colour, movement, details such as pearl headed pins and of course the character of the Gloriosa all crave our attention.

53

Bon Appetit!

Designer
Max
Materials
Fritillaria imperialis / Crown imperial
Lepidum sativum/ Garden cress
Papaver nudicaule / Iceland poppy
Ranunculus (mixed) / Turban buttercup
Tulipa / tulip
oasis
plastic foil
red fruits (berries, strawberries, tomatoes)
tea light candles
tissue/blotting paper

1 Place plastic foil and tissue paper on a round table that is provided with cut-outs for oasis. Fill the table with oasis. Dampen the tissue/blotting paper and sow garden cress. Make sure you leave sufficient room for crockery and cutlery. Sprinkle and leave to grow!

2 During the next seven days, leave the garden cress to shoot at room temperature. Water every day!

3 Place tea light candles and dishes with strawberries, tomatoes and red berries on the table.

4 Insert flowers in the oasis amongst the garden cress. Do this in a very natural, casual manner and start with the largest flowers. Work with the round shapes of the table.

5 The same goes for fruit decoration: repeat the same curves of the table on the plates too.

Design This design offers a complete picture: the table, the food and the decorations are one, fuse with one another and complement each other, where necessary.
Technique If necessary, make an extra wooden table top that you place on top of an existing table. Take your time with the garden cress and keep the base sufficiently moist at all times. Good planning is essential!
Emotion This modern table of green garden cress flows into the flower section and blends in with the fruits in a natural and casual way. This arrangement creates a total atmosphere, a separate world. Materials, design and scents guarantee a fantastic dinner.

Flowering eggs

Designer
Per

Materials
Acacia floribunda / Gossamer wattle
Craspedia globosa / golden drumstick
Gerbera mini / daisy
Narcissus 'Tête-à-Tête' / daffodil
Ranunculus / buttercup
eggs
egg cups
floral fix
feathers
glue and hot glue gun

Design Decorative arrangement, a bit naïve and childlike but perfectly fitting the spring theme. Make use of what is available and play along; eggs are the main theme in the bases, colours and expressions on the table and the plates.

Technique Arranging technique for flowers and bulbs, combined with gluing for the bulbs and floral fix to stabilize the eggs in the cups. For stability reasons it is recommended to fill the eggs with lots of water.

Emotions What is Easter, if not about eggs, eggs and even more eggs! The colour is yellow, spanning from a pale egg white to the deepest warm and sunny yellow. It is a time to be happy and joyful, to celebrate with flowering eggs!

Flowering eggs

1 Collect all materials: egg cups, eggs and flowers in a wide spectrum of yellow.
Empty the eggs (burdening you with omelettes for more than a week!), clean the shells and let them dry.

2 Use well-watered daffodils, separate them, clean them of soil and most of the roots and let them dry slightly. Put one bulb in the centre of each egg and secure it with glue to prevent if from falling when out of balance.

3 Clean away all foliage from the flowers and cut them in the desired lengths. Use those eggs that have smaller holes and fill them with water, place them in the egg cups and arrange the flowers into them. The weight of the water is needed for stability.

4 Mix and match different egg cups as well as bulbs and cut flowers to create a decorative irregular expression in the final design. If the eggs still keep slipping inside the cups, use some flower fix to secure them.

5 Arrange all egg cups in a crossed pattern, creating a long trailing rectangular shape along the table much like a tablecloth or a flower carpet. Finish the design with some feathers and egg-shaped candles.

58

5

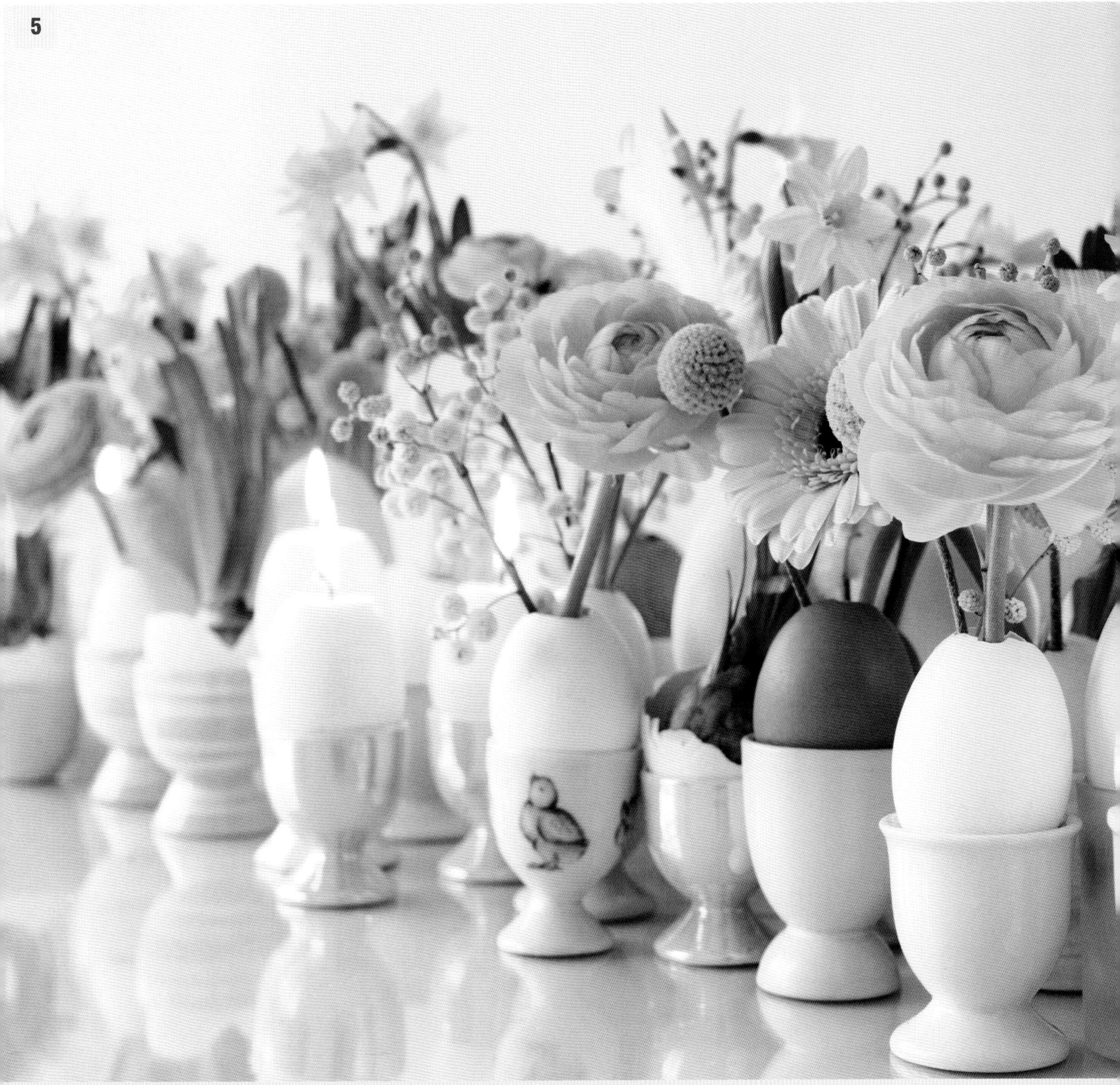

Helleborus in style

Designer
Tomas
Materials
Helleborus
Larix decidua / larch (twigs covered in moss)
Pilea
Glass tubes
Glue gun
Metal base
polystyrene
silver twine
small Christmas baubles
spray paint (grey)
spray snow
wool

Design A Christmas table without warmth is incomplete. The cosy wintry atmosphere is evoked by the use of colour and materials. The dark and stylish, yet warm grey base accommodates the vulnerable *Helleborus*. The Christmas baubles add extra festivity and a dusting of spray snow finishes it off.

Technique A multi-functional metal base and a polystyrene holder make up the base of this arrangement. The twigs are held in place with hot glue. Since the larch twigs cannot possibly conceal the polystyrene, first spray it grey and wrap it in wool in order to create an organic camouflage.

Emotions A cosy, yet stylish Christmas table. The flowers seem like extra guests in the room: they demand nothing from us, ask nothing in return for their presence, but instead let us enjoy their beautiful simplicity.

1 A sturdy metal base and a polystyrene holder make up the base of this arrangement. The Larix twigs offer the flowers a comfortable and warm shelter.

2 To cover up the base, first spray it grey and wrap it in coarse wool. As well as making the polystyrene invisible, this will help glue down the twigs covered in moss more effectively.

3 First tie glass tubes to the arrangement. Spread them equally across the arrangement. Then glue down the twigs. Do not glue them flat on top of one another but leave the necessary transparency, giving the arrangement depth without coming across as bulky or too compact.

4 Place the flowers in the tubes. Spread the flowers creatively. Do not place too many in one spot or spread them too evenly. Avoid a field of flowers, but rather let the Helleborus flowers speak for themselves. They give this arrangement class, personality and beauty.

Growing together

Designer
Max
Materials
Betula / Birch
Fritillaria (mixed) / Fritillary
Ranunculus (mixed) / Turban buttercup
Tulipa (mixed) / Tulip
tulip vases

1 Spread the 10 vases across the length of the table, not symmetrically or in one line, but in two lines. Create a balance in doing so. Fill up the vases with water.

2 Carefully defoliate the flowers, so as to end up with smooth stalks. Leave the odd top leaf on the stalk of the tulips; otherwise the arrangement could appear too sterile.

3 Distribute the Betula across the vases as if it were one arrangement. Do not only give due consideration to the Betula's direction of growth, but also respect the linear direction of the vases and the table.

4 Now distribute the other flowers across the vases, starting with the tulips. Leave them to fall and grow quite naturally. Do not make things too rigid or too forced and pay attention to the direction the vases are facing. Add the smallest flowers last.

Design Inspired by the tulip vases of yesteryear, in which the flowers were arranged quite naturally and with movement. In these more stylised vases, we are slightly more rigid but are keen to retain the old casual look.
Technique The flowers have quite simply been put in water, but give due consideration to the movement of the materials. Make sure everything is steeped in water.
Emotion The casual charm, the movement and colours of the flowers give this arrangement a nostalgic twist; a drive towards downshifting in these hectic times and our busy lives.

63

Christmas red

Designer
Per
Materials
Ilex verticillata / common winterberry
Picea abies / Norway spruce
Pinus / pine
Pinus (fruit) / pine cones
foam wreath
glass candle holders
stub wire (19 gauge)
Mizuhiki wire

Design A Christmas wreath that uses traditional colours and materials, but is modern, simple and clean in its expression. This arrangement shows that there is still place for flowers in our modern-time Christmas celebrations.
Technique Normal foam and wiring techniques, executed with precision and accuracy. If you want your wreath to last all Christmas season, make sure to use fresh, well-watered pines and spruce twigs.
Emotions Warmth, candles, traditional materials, red, green and brown... They all have been associated with Christmas for ages and bring to mind the carefree and peaceful Christmas days of our childhood.

1 Assort all materials and start by wiring the cut pieces of Ilex and the pine cones. Use normal stub wire for the cones and red (or any other colour) Mizuhiki wire for the Ilex, since that wire will be visible.

2 Place the small, short pine and spruce branches into the foam, creating a slightly domed outer profile. Work vertically on the inside. Glue the branches to the plastic part of the wreath where needed.

3 The wired pine cones are placed on a straight horizontal line all around the wreath. Make sure to save enough space in between them for putting the candle holders.

4 Finally place the candle holders in an irregular rhythm and fill in the gaps with the wired Ilex berries. Make sure all foam is covered. Where needed put some spruce underneath the Ilex berries. Use some beautiful weathered pine branches as a final touch, softening the expression.

65

Closed up

Designer
Max
Materials
Fritillaria meleagris / Snake's Head Fritillary
Narcissus / Daffodil
Nerine bowdenii
Prunus persica / Peach
Ranunculus / Turban buttercup
Rosa / Rose
Tulipa / Tulip
Zantedeschia / Calla lily
PVC (3 colours)
pink twine
stapler

1 Cut the PVC into squares of three different sizes and staple them together to make up squares with a surface area that matches that of the circumference of the glass dishes. Make sure the colours are spread unevenly, but are still balanced.

2 Unwind two bobbins of twine across the length of the dishes, all in one go. These are hooked together so as to create a sturdy construction for inserting flowers later on.

3 Place the construction in the dish and fill it with water. Next, place the heavier materials in the vase, parallel to one another, and tie them together, where necessary. Make up the two dishes at the same time so as to obtain uniformity.

4 Now simply insert the other flowers in the construction, each flower parallel to the next. Every flower species has its own tier so that the arrangement has a natural look.

Design By combining the unnatural PVC with the frivolous, natural flowers, a very contemporary arrangement is created.
Technique What is different is that coloured thread is used on a transparent basis. This is an excellent substitute for oasis. By using plastic, many existing backgrounds can be given a totally different look.
Emotion A business-like arrangement with some frivolity thrown in. Suitable for business meetings, for example.

67

Joyful simplicity

Designer
Per
Materials
Craspedia globosa / golden drumstick
Phormium / New Zealand flax
Ranunculus / buttercup
glass candle holders
Mizuhiki wire (soft and hard)
pearl-headed pins
pearls

Design Joyful springtime design that is all about circles, from the candle holders, the Phormium and flowers to the accessories. Simplicity in materials and colours puts emphasis on the beautiful Ranunculus.
Technique Instead of floral foam we use botanical materials as a natural support for the flowers. Many spring flowers, such as Ranunculus, do not last very long in foam; therefore this technique is a respectful and easy alternative for these flowers.
Emotions Those bubbly, sparkling, joyful spring feelings that are awoken by the warmth and sunshine after a long winter are all present in this arrangement. Feelings that make us smile and give a rosy picture of life. I hope this arrangement has the same effect on the table guests.

1 Collect a nice variety of flowers in pastel colours, ranging from orange to pink. Select strong as well as soft colours to create tension in the arrangement.

2 Start by making rolls of Phormium leaves and place them in water-filled candle holders in the same variety of colours as the flowers. Make sure the rolls, once inside the candle holders, open up as much as to be secured, rising some 2 cm above the edge.

3 Put the flowers in between the layers of the rolled Phormium leaves, well-secured and slightly above the edge. Adjust the amount of flowers in each container according to their sizes.

4 Finally place the accessories, the soft and the hard Mizuhiki wires, some with, others without pearls, circling on the inside and outside of the table arrangement. Pierce the wires into the Craspedia and use them as a technical support.

A playful Easter table

Designer
Tomas

Materials
Diplocyclos palmatus / whip vine
Jasminum polyanthum / jasmine
Ranunculus asiaticus / turban buttercup
Viburnum opulus / Guelder rose
Viburnum tinus 'Eve price'
aluminium dish
glue gun
goose eggs

Design The attractive shape and texture of the dish give this arrangement an elegant look. The goose eggs add a playful touch and are in keeping with the Easter theme. By using the colourful flowers and the predominantly white crockery and table linen, we create a playful, elegant style.
Technique The vase creates a basic shape in which we glue the eggshells in place. We use hot glue for this. Do not forget to glue the eggshells together for extra fixation. Although we use the eggshells as individual receptacles for the many flowers, this functional element will be interpreted as purely decorative by the dinner guests.
Emotions The colourful flowers add a striking note to this predominantly austere, white table decoration and form the focal point of the table. The flowers, with their individuality and personality, speak for themselves, just as every dinner guest has his/her own voice and personality.

1 We opt for a broad, yet harmonious colour palette, ranging from pastel pink, through purple and orange to soft green. These colours go well with the aluminium colour of the receptacle. The Diplocyclos gives an extra touch to the arrangement. We prefer larger goose eggs as water reservoirs for the flowers.

2 Take the top off a few eggs. The shape of the dish determines the line of the arrangement. We can use a glue gun to glue the eggs in place. Glue the eggs to each other for extra sturdiness. Alternate the open sides of the eggs to the left and right of the dish so that the dinner guests on both sides of the table can enjoy the flower arrangement.

3 First place a few Diplocyclos vines between the eggs as a green background. The green berries with white stripes link the flowers and the white eggs but also add a discrete playfulness to the table arrangement.

4 We can now add the flowers. Fill the eggs with water first. Start with the Ranunculus and mix the colours well when placing them in the dish. Inserting flowers in between the Diplocyclos twigs increases the coherence of the arrangement.

5 To break the compactness of the arrangement, we place a few fluid lines of Jasminum, as this relaxes the arrangement.

Robust

Designer
Max

Materials
Amaranthus caudatus / Love lies bleeding
Astrantia major /Masterwort
Cynara scolymus / Artichoke
Dianthus / Carnation
Gloriosa rothschildiana / Glory lily
Rosa / Rose
Syringa vulgaris / Lilac
Tulipa / Tulip
Oasis
test tubes
2 vases (see picture)

Design A contained table arrangement with height. This is placed on the side of the table so as not to disturb the guests. Work at one height with heavy, robust flower shapes. The leaf-less stalks that stick out from this abstract vase add elegance and character.

Technique Test tubes are used to achieve height that cannot be obtained otherwise. It is also important to treat the oasis properly.

Emotion The stalks that come from this abstract vase and blend in with the heavy flowers, and the colours give this arrangement a retro feeling. This has been a recurring theme in designs in very many areas recently.

1 Fill up the vases with oasis. First, allow the oasis to soak up plenty of water and cut to the right size. Do not squeeze the oasis in a hole (that is too small), as this affects the structure of the materials and prevents it from absorbing water.

2 Extend the test tubes with pieces of lilac wood. In that way, a few flowers can be placed higher in the arrangement. The lilac wood will no longer be noticeable in the vases.

3 Create two identical constructions with lilac in the vases. Remove most leaves from all flowers. Do not be too strict: the odd leaf will add a playful touch.

4 Add the flowers, starting at the top and working your way down. First, use the heavy artichoke and make an outline with the Amaranthus. The arrangement is given height thanks to the extended test tubes. Then, add the other flowers. In doing so, heed the shape (see photograph) and the parallel lines of the stalks.

73

Mysteriously dark

Designer
Per

Materials
Betula / birch
Salix / willow
Tulipa / tulip
cable ties
metal container

Design This work focuses on the colour black: the combination of the rigid metal container, the natural but man-made Betula structure (following the rectangular shape of the container) and the wild, mysterious dark tulips.
Technique Arranging technique with Betula support replacing the traditional floral foam, binding technique with cable ties and some weaving with the tulips. Remember the importance of clean Betula to avoid bacteria and dirt in the water.
Emotions The ever thrilling mystery of darkness and black, which traps us in both positive and negative ways. This arrangement is all about the positive side of darkness, represented by the tulip.

1 Rinse the Betula and Salix properly and clear the tulips of all but their smallest leaves. To make the weaving easier and to get more curving, put the tulips aside without water for a couple of hours before use.

2 When making the actual structure it is important to use carefully washed Betula. Rinse them with hot water and a dish brush, to avoid bacteria in the water later on. Make a measuring stick, cut all Betula stems accordingly and put them parallely inside the container. Don't pack them too tightly to allow arranging flowers in between the twigs.

3 Use Salix and cable ties to create a transparent structure on top of the Betula that will support the tulips. Arrange the tulips in between the Betula and connect them in a crisscross pattern.

4 Finally arrange the tulips, starting from where you want the actual flower head, weaving in between the Salix and pushing them in between the Betula. Work in both directions and overlap to achieve movement and life in the final design.

75

Pure!

Designer
Tomas

Materials
Papaver nudicaule / Iceland poppy
Xerophyllum tenax / bear grass
acrylic sheet
double-walled polycarbonate cavity sheet
flower gel (granules)
silicon (glue)

Design This design fits in perfectly in a modern, loft-type, or minimalist Zen interior. The simplicity and elegance will immediately catch the eye of the dinner guests. This striking austerity is obtained by use of colour, transparent acrylic, polycarbonate and flower gel, but also by applying a simple and honest arranging technique.

Technique The double-walled polycarbonate sheet gives us small receptacles, which enables us to use the flowers on their own. The gel gives the poppies enough water and its transparency allows us to work very openly and honestly. An 'honest technique' that allows complete transparency and insight into the working method used and into the management of material.

Emotions With this table arrangement, we evoke a sense of purity and design. The simple enjoyment of the beauty, development and honesty of these flowers. Pure enjoyment of each other's company.

PURE!

1 *Less is more* is the core theme underlying this arrangement. Hence the use of just one flower species: the poppy. This flower is sufficiently powerful and has enough personality and shape to be used on its own. We place three high-grade polycarbonate cavity sheets on an acrylic sheet. These cavity sheets are normally used as roof covering for conservatories, car ports, pergolas, etc. According to its thickness (4 to 32 mm), this sheet is single- or double-walled.

2 As a base, we use an acrylic sheet of 100 by 20 cm on which we place three double-walled polycarbonate cavity sheets. To create volume, we use 3 different dimensions: a first plate of 60 by 10 cm, a second of 45 by 14 cm and finally a plate of 75 by 12 cm. These are attached with silicone glue. Make sure the acrylic sheet is free from grease to ensure proper fixation.

3 Fill all the cavities with flower gel granules, but not all to the same level or up to the edge, as this will add an extra dimension and an element of playfulness to the floral arrangement.

4 Place the flowers very carefully. Respect their growing direction and take their colour and stage of development into consideration. Create a harmonious arrangement by allowing fluidity between them. The thin double wall of the polycarbonate will keep the flowers firmly in place. A good exercise in sensing, and listening to,

the flowers' individuality.

All tangled up

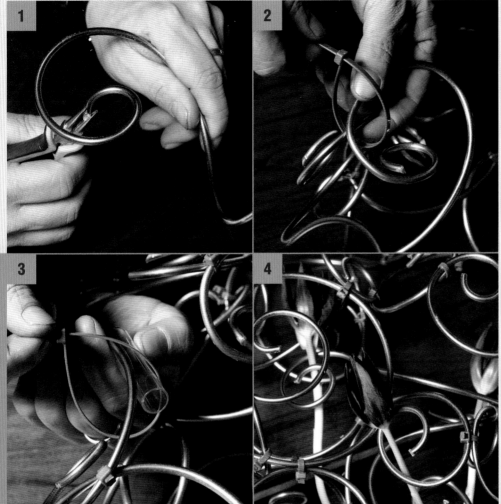

Designer
Max
Materials
Hedera helix / Ivy
Ranunculus / Turban buttercup
Tulipa / Tulip
aluminium wire (6mm)
red cable ties
test tubes

Design The design takes its inspiration from the way in which vines naturally intertwine and create a world and atmosphere of their own. Even though the vines are replaced here by aluminium wire, the arrangement gives the same impression.

Technique The frame should not give you any problems if the aluminium wire has been curved properly. Make sure sufficient depth and space are created for the flowers and that the tubes can hold sufficient water for the flowers.

Emotion The gripping movements of the materials give off a natural force, as if they are still growing. This makes for a relaxed and modern creation.

1 Cut pink aluminium wire in pieces of about 60 cm and use a pair of pliers to curl up the ends.

2 Intertwine the pieces of wire. Use pink cable ties to keep the wires firmly in place. Cut off any ends so as not to break up the curvy creation.

3 Drape over the corner of a table and make sure it is sits well. Make sure there is enough depth in the frame. Now attach the test tubes with cable ties, making sure that enough water can stay in them.

4 Strip the leaves from the ivy, the tulips and the turban buttercups, so that you end up with nice, smooth stalks. Interlace these in the frame by following the movement of the aluminium wire. Make sure all flowers can get enough water.

81

Springtime fakir

Designer
Per
Materials
Crocus
Fritillaria meleagris / snake's head fritillary
Muscari / grape hyacinth
Narcissus 'Tête-à-Tête' / daffodil
drill
hammer
measuring stick
nails
spray paint
wooden plank

Design The contrast between the fragility of the flowers
and the aggressiveness of the sharp nails creates tension
and excitement. A very subtle and at the same time strong
way to emphasize the fragility of the spring flowers.
Technique Piercing technique in an innovative and
effective way. The bulbs do very good without their soil
when well watered before use. For longer durability they
can be sprayed from time to time.
Emotions Contrasts explain most things to us in life.
Love is explained by sorrow, strength by weakness,
beauty by ugliness, light by darkness... The tender
fragile beauty of the flowering bulbs is explained
through the strong and sharp metal of the nails.

83

Springtime fakir

1 In this design the actual preparation of the structure takes quite some time, while the flower part is less time-consuming. The good news is that the structure can be reused afterwards.

2 Choose a wooden plank according to the width and the length of the table. Measure and draw a pattern according to which you drill holes. Drill from the top side (best side). Be precise and make sure all holes are straight.

3 Paint the plank – if wanted – before hammering in the nails. The nails are hammered in from below and exit the wood on what will become the top side.

4 Slightly trim the different flowering bulbs, well watered from the start and cleaned from soil and roots. To get interesting curves on the flowers, lay them flat on a surface for a day before use.

5 Pierce the bulbs onto the nails and use the fakir bed to angle and curve the flower stems even more. Work in all directions to create a livelier pattern similar to the power and movement of spring.

6 Push the bulbs halfway down on the nails, be careful not to break them. Work out a volume, but keep the nails clean and visible to make it look as if the bulbs are floating on top of the nails.

Less is more

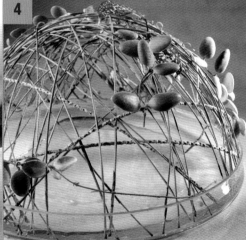

Designer
Tomas
Materials
Adiantum raddianum / Maidenhair fern
Ceropegia woodii ssp. / Sweetheart vine
Dischidia nummularia
Dracaena godseffiana / Gold dust Dracaena
Hoya linearis
Nolina / Elephant's foot
Phalaenopsis / Moth orchid
Phoenix canariensis / Canary Island date palm (dried)
mikado sticks
silver-coloured thread

Design A voluminous design which is not too heavy on the eye thanks to its transparent construction. A balancing act! The flowers flutter, as it were, through and among the mesh and add a sense of calm to the table. The table decoration has been kept very sober with earthy colours, natural table cloths, coarse plates, etc. The wooden Mikado sticks blend in perfectly.
Technique The main difficulty is creating a symmetrical construction. All you need to do is to place a few sticks securely in the vase and tie them together carefully. Once these are firmly in place, you can start weaving. You will need a dish with raised edges.
Emotions These earthy colours and natural materials conjure up a sense of connectedness with Mother Earth and Creation. Satisfaction, stability and inner strength are the core emotions in this table arrangement.

1 We opt for natural materials with an exotic twist. The Mikado sticks and dried Phoenix are sufficiently flexible to create the hemisphere. The greenery can be delicate as it is in direct contact with water. We would advise you not to make things difficult for yourself, so opt for a dish with raised edges.

2 By tying together at least 15 Mikado sticks, a domed structure can be created. Tie the sticks down with twine so that they cannot become undone. In this arrangement, we use the strength and elasticity of the sticks in the dish to give the dome its shape. This provides stability and a firm base in which to weave in the other sticks.

3 We can now carefully build the perfect dome construction. Make sure you weave as neatly as possible, for the better the weaving, the more striking the result. Finish off by adding a few Phoenix twigs to break up the uniformity.

4 Start by adding the other greenery. A line pattern can be determined by means of the Nolina, for example. The large Dracaena leaf adds a sense of calm to the arrangement.

5 Finish off with flowers and a few Adiantum leaves. The Hoya linearis and the Ceropegia form the finishing touch and give the arrangement a special feel.

Frosted winter whites

Designer
Per

Materials
Betula / birch
Helleborus niger / Christmas rose
Salix / willow
big needle
fake ice crystals
feathers
glass container
Styrofoam
white stub wires

1 For this arrangement we need materials that express a winter feel: Styrofoam, white feathers, plastic crystals, branches and the adorable Helleborus. Start by cutting a round plate from Styrofoam as a flower support and as a top for the glass container.

2 Cut the branches in shorter pieces of the same length and wire them onto white painted stub wires or silver Mizuhiki wires.

3 Put water in the container and place the Styrofoam top into position. Make sure it is tight enough to stay in place when working flowers through it. Place all wired branches in a crossed pattern as a transparent upper surface and flower support. Add feathers by tying or weaving them into the surface.

4 The Helleborus are pierced through the Styrofoam with the help of a big pin and are pushed through later on. The stems will be supported by the Styrofoam and the flower heads by the transparent web of branches and twigs.

5 Add feathers in between the flower heads and some more thin branches where needed to achieve the desired transparency. Add some fake frost crystals for that final touch!

Design Transparent both in colour as in materials, this arrangement projects lightness, light, purity and silence just as those winter mornings when the landscape is covered with the first snow and the damp is changing into a crisp cold. A perfect combination with the only winter flowerer: the Helleborus!

Technique A layer of Styrofoam is used instead of floral foam, to give transparency and to allow clear water in the container, which is much better for the Helleborus. Make the Styrofoam plate slightly bigger than the hole of the container to have it stay in place.

Emotions A winter morning, peaceful and quiet, everything dusted in snow and white trees covered with frost… When looking really close you will notice a whole universe of different snow crystals.

Romantic union

Designer
Tomas
Materials
Calamus rotang / pulp cane
Ceropegia woodii ssp. / sweetheart vine
Prunus serrulata / oriental cherry
Rosa sp. / rose flower
Salix / willow
Xanthorrhoea australis / Grass tree
Oasis (ordinary Oasis and Oasis Rainbow Powder)

Design By placing the dishes rhythmically, not only do
we create a harmonious unity, we also add strength to
the arrangement. The austere design is softened by the
pastel pink roses, by adding Prunus and by the coloured
pulp cane which also adds transparency. An austere,
male base, finished off with a soft, feminine touch.
Technique Our basic shape is created by the parallel
arches formed by the twigs, alternately inserted from
the left and right hand side of the receptacle. The twigs
are clamped between the container's two upright sides
and inserted in oasis, which also provides the water for
all the plants. The coloured Oasis Rainbow powder adds
a decorative finish to the green oasis.
Emotions The salmon pink roses instantly create a
pleasant, romantic atmosphere. The restrained use
of colour and the soft feminine curves guarantee a
relaxed and informal get-together.

Romantic union

1 A sturdy container and fresh flexible Salix twigs make up the austere basic shape of this arrangement. Roses, Ceropegia, Prunus and soft pink pulp cane add a refined romantic touch.

2 Place the oasis in the dish and cover it with a coating of coloured oasis powder. Not only does this look more attractive, the softness of the powder forms a striking contrast with the rigid construction of the Salix twigs. Place the twigs, starting alternately on the left-hand side and right-hand side of the container. This variation ensures that the tension across the length of the arch is distributed and the highest point is central.

3 Carefully place the roses in the arrangement. This may appear easy, but bear in mind that the flower heads should be visible to all dinner guests. Place each rose in a way that it 'smiles' or 'glances' at a dinner guest. This is essential. Allow your flowers to communicate with the dinner guests. Take sufficient time to do this!

4 Once all the flowers are put in place, we add some transparency by bending some coloured pulp cane over the Salix twigs. The fresh green colour of the Xanthorrhoea australis exudes calmness, while the Ceropegia vines soften everything and add an element of romance.

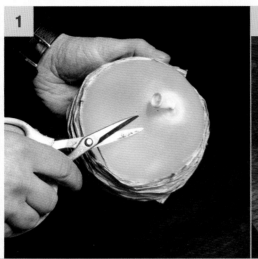

Natural spring

Designer
Max
Materials
Convallaria majalis / Lily of the valley
Galanthus nivalis (bulb) / Snowdrops (bulb)
Muscari (bulb) / Grape hyacinth (bulb)
Narcissus 'Zivz' (bulb) / Daffodil (bulb)
Sphagnum
balloons
raffia
transparent plastic
wallpaper paste

Design Organically formed dishes of raffia planted with flower bulbs are a minimalist and pure table decoration.
Technique Make up the base as described and make sure that the air is not released from the balloons until the raffia is completely dry. Allow the plants to drink plenty before being planted up; they will not need much water later on.
Emotion Fresh, pure, minimalist and at the same time optimistic and noble. The arrangement exudes a sense of calm.

1 Make up the wallpaper paste to twice the prescribed thickness and blow up the balloons to the desired size. Dunk the raffia into the paste and wrap it very carefully around the balloons. Repeat this again and leave everything to dry at room temperature for two days.

2 Carefully pierce the balloons and slowly let the air escape. Place transparent plastic in the raffia baskets.

3 Allow the plants and flower bulbs to soak up plenty of water and plant these in the raffia baskets on their own. Do not use potting soil for planting, but *Sphagnum* instead. Decorate the table with the raffia baskets.

Future, creations & step-by-step instructions
Per Benjamin (SE)
Max van de Sluis (NL)
Tomas De Bruyne (BE)

History
Per Benjamin (SE)

Drawings
Kathy van de Sluis-Kim (NL)

Photography
Kurt Dekeyzer (BE)
Helén Pe (SE)
Pim van der Maden (NL)

Translation
Taal-Ad-Visie, Brugge (BE)

Final Editing
Katrien Van Moerbeke

Layout and print
Group Van Damme, Oostkamp (BE)

Published by
Stichting Kunstboek bvba
Legeweg 165
B-8020 Oostkamp
Belgium
tel. +32 50 46 19 10
fax +32 50 46 19 18
info@stichtingkunstboek.com
www.stichtingkunstboek.com

ISBN: 978-90-5856-323-1
D/2009/6407/25
NUR: 421

Per

Max

Tomas

a bundle of creativity www.life3.net

Life3 is an international partnership consisting of
Per Benjamin, Max van de Sluis and Tomas De Bruyne.
Per started working with flowers at an early age,
almost by accident, and now has his own consulting
companies, Benjamins Botaniska in Stockholm. Tomas
is a floral designer who brightens up events and
happenings worldwide. He has a consulting companies
in Belgium and is an internationally established value.

They have all worked in various fields of the flower
industry, ranging from nurseries, wholesalers and retail
shops, and each of them is devoted to both commercial
and artistic designs focusing on the emotional side of
flowers. Per, Max and Tomas value the importance of
training and give demonstrations and classes all around
the world as well as in their home countries.

Per, Max and Tomas have taken part in many
competitions and have won several medals both
nationally and internationally. At the 2002 World Cup in
the Netherlands they were first, third and fifth
(respectively Per, Max and Tomas). In the aftermath
of the competition, they ended up talking and
commenting each other's works. Once they got talking,
they started playing with the idea of working together
in the future. It soon became clear that they shared the
same ideas and visions. Only half a year later, Life3
was born.

Life3 stands for emotions, creativity, craftsmanship
and communication. This partnership, the first of its
kind between three florists, aims to add new value to
the flower industry. It wants to take floral design up to
new levels and wishes to bring it to a wider audience.
Life3 offers demonstrations, workshops, decorations,
shows, seminars and books – both educational and
purely inspirational – and education for small and big
groups. They offer trend information, product design
and development, everything within the world of
flowers and beyond.